A Thousand Paths to Comfort

A Thousand Paths to
comfort

David Baird

MQP

Contents

Introduction

Who, with hand on heart, can say that they are completely comfortable with themselves, let alone with their life? Some of us are uncomfortable with our jobs, our homes, or in the company of certain people. Some of us will have faced, or are facing, difficult periods in life. In truth, most of us want and seek comfort in our life, yet many of us seem to believe that it can only be achieved through wealth or success. But comfort cannot be measured through material possessions. It is more about a feeling, a contract that we draw up between our thoughts, our actions, and ourselves. And it can enter our lives the moment we set about making sense of the role we play in the infinite structure of things.

In this book, old voices mingle with new thoughts in an attempt to gain a fresh perspective on what it means to be comfortable, and to offer the inspiration to set out along the many paths that lead to comfort.

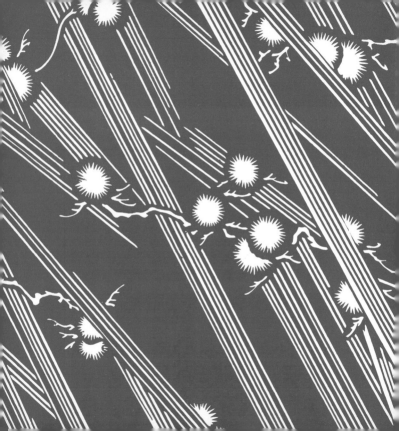

Comforting
Thoughts

We are the spice of life. Sometimes we need to be trodden upon in order to release our full fragrance.

Some of us see the glass as half empty—others see it as half full. Those who choose to see a world full of suffering should realize that it is also a world full of people overcoming their suffering.

We shall overcome.

Why wait for some extraordinary circumstances to do good action?
Use ordinary situations.
Use the moment.

There is more comfort in doing what you can than in doing nothing at all.

Where you are, with what you have, do what you can.

We become wiser by adversity; prosperity destroys our appreciation of the right.

Seneca

Look at age as opportunity.

When we are true to nature we can be comfortable with our age.

The best part of beauty is that which no picture can express.

Francis Bacon

The greatest battles we shall ever face are with ourselves—overcoming desire is a far greater achievement than overcoming foes.

There is nobody with no redeeming features.

We are, in a sense, our own worst enemy.

Be patient— you cannot see the stars until it gets dark.

Be good.

Be kind.

Be humane.

Be charitable.

Console the afflicted.

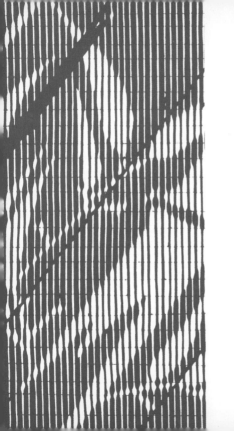

If we are ready to forgive, forgiveness can precede an apology.

A round man cannot be expected to fit in a square hole right away. He must have time to modify his shape.

Mark Twain

What is more comforting than seeing two people who, after being locked in dispute, reach agreement?

To all, to each, a fair good-night, And pleasing dreams, and slumbers light.

Sir Walter Scott

Truth is generally kindness, but where the two diverge and collide, kindness should override truth.

Samuel Butler

Do not judge yourself more harshly than you judge others.

We can't reach for the stars with others holding us down.

Laughter is the soul's champagne.

Never underestimate the power of a smile.

Never underestimate the power of a few comforting words.

Never underestimate the power of a comforting touch.

Never underestimate the power of listening to others.

Never underestimate the power of an honest compliment.

Never underestimate the power of showing that you care.

The wonderful thing about human beings is that we each possess the ability to turn someone else's life around for the better.

Some people want absolutely everything in life only to discover that they have nowhere to put it all.

Making promises is fine and wonderful, but only if you intend to keep them.

One should not stand at the foot of a sick person's bed, because that place is reserved for the guardian angel.

Jewish folk saying

The most comfortable person is busy caring for someone else's comfort.

Take the care out of the community and the community disintegrates.

The best and most
wonderful things in this life
cannot be seen or touched.
They must be felt.

Inside every
rocky heart is an
angel waiting to
be set free.

When all you can see is gloomy and
life is in shadow, turn around
and face the sun.

**When we have a sense of humor
we can feel comfortable about
anything that life throws at us.
Without it we are at its mercy.**

For comfort's sake it is probably best to
believe the best of people until they
themselves prove us to be wrong.

It is a curious fact that when we go out of our way to make life more comfortable for others, our own life becomes more comfortable too.

You may feel your contribution to life is a mere drop in the ocean, but remove it and the level will fall.

**When you think you can,
you are right.**

When you think you can't,
you are right.

**Take pleasure from the
past, but live in the now.**

We can all find a hundred reasons daily to do mischief, but there are always twice as many to do good.

I count him braver who overcomes his desires than him who conquers his enemies; for the hardest victory is over self.

Aristotle

Try the untried— that's where discovery is.

Don't seek comfort purely from those who agree with you.

I take great comfort from the fact that I am always able to laugh at myself before anyone else laughs at me.

Life is not really complicated at all. When we can adopt a simple view of life then we can get into it and on with it.

No joy should be deemed too small to pass unacknowledged.

The greatest thing anyone can ever grow is a lasting friendship.

The best thing we can possibly pass on to the next generation is some ability.

The pessimist feels the wind and fears a hurricane.

The optimist feels the wind and waits for the change.

Comfortable people feel the wind and fly their kites.

Tomorrow is always new.

**No person can get by on charm
alone without some knowledge.**

No person can get by on
knowledge alone without
some charm.

**Those who are dishonest
cannot feel insults.**

Those who are honest
do not fear insults.

Who is comfortable saying
what ought to be said, when
in truth they have something
of their own to say?

Sit in reverie, and watch the changing color of the waves that break upon the idle seashore of the mind.

Henry Wadsworth Longfellow

Even if it is only for a moment, we are all geniuses at some point in our lives.

Those fashionable youths who see you and scorn you as old-fashioned will be laughed at for the same reasons one day.

Who cannot be comfortable in the knowledge that they are loved?

We can
always
comply
while
holding
on to our
opinion.

Those who cannot feel comfortable being of any nationality can always take comfort in being a member of the human race.

Nobody can manage a fool.

No matter how a person dresses, they should be judged by their ability.

When we have a clear mind and clarity of vision we can be definite in what we do and say.

If it gives you comfort, you can always wait and hope.

I think, therefore I am.
René Descartes

When our lives are filled with uncertainty, we leave no time for anything else.

Everyone thinks his own cross is the heaviest.

When you are under a lot of pressure, imagine yourself to be made of coal—that way you will emerge a diamond.

Be comforted by the thought that if you had everything you desire there would be nothing to look forward to.

Be comforted by the thought that everything that you don't know is an opportunity to learn.

Be comforted by the thought that without difficult times there would be no easier times.

Be comforted by the thought that each new challenge builds your strength and character.

How can we be courageous
if we are never scared?

**Belief prevails when
humanity fails.**

Friendship is
what bonds the
world together.

A dog cannot lie. If only humans had tails too, then we'd really know whether or not someone is happy to see us.

The best mirror on our life is an old friend.

We are comfortable when we can get as much joy in solitude as in company.

You cannot see eye to eye with someone you look down on.

Certain thoughts are prayers. There are moments when, whatever be the attitude of the body, the soul is on its knees.

Victor Hugo

Let us dare to live our life as we understand it.

Do not waste a lifetime by trying to banish all danger. Just spend a moment now and then to banish fear.

The Lord is nigh unto them that are of a broken heart; and saveth such as be of a contrite spirit.

Psalms 34:18

The path from bondage leads
to spiritual truth.

**The path from spiritual truth
leads to great courage.**

The path from great courage
leads to liberty.

The path from liberty leads to abundance.

The path from abundance leads to selfishness.

Selfishness leads us
to complacency.

Complacency leads us to apathy.

Apathy leads us to dependence.

Dependence leads us to bondage.

What lies behind us
and what lies before
us are tiny matters,
compared to what lies
within us.

Ralph Waldo Emerson

It is our differences that make us interesting.

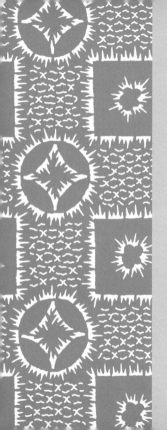

The level of comfort we seek defines the direction our lives will take.

The easy way is rarely the best.

Who in their own lifetime will recognize, let alone understand, their own completeness?

Thinking is easy, acting is difficult.

To put one's thoughts into action is the most difficult thing in the world.
Johann Wolfgang von Goethe

**It may offend us to hear our own
thoughts expressed by others:
we are not sure enough of their souls.**

Jean Rostand

We destroy what is with
thoughts of what may be.

Only man clogs his
happiness with care.
John Dryden

Adolescence is enough
suffering for anyone.

A hen is an egg's way of
creating another egg.
Samuel Butler

Be like the bird that, halting on its flight
Awhile on boughs too slight,
Feels them give way beneath her,
and yet sings
Knowing that she hath wings.

Victor Hugo

All life is circular—you see things turn out best for those who make the best of the way things turn out.

Things are
are and no
them to b

**Nothing ra
book. It ins
encourage**

Comfort is feeling
safe in someone's
presence.

A good laugh is like sunshine. It can drive away the darkness.

Life looks better
when you smile.

**It is sad but true, we are not as
important as we think we are.**

Everything you
need to be you,
you already have.

Anger will never disappear so long as thoughts of resentment are cherished in the mind.

Anger will disappear just as soon as thoughts of resentment are forgotten.

Buddha

Everything in
Perspective

Be comforted by the thought that each mistake we make in life is an opportunity to learn a valuable lesson.

Be comforted by the thought
that being tired and weary
is usually a sign of having
achieved something.

**Accept that life is filled
with setbacks and you will
doubly appreciate the good
things that it has to offer.**

Since man first walked this earth, love and truth have always prevailed, regardless of the threats that confronted him.

Troubles have a knack of melting away when we turn the negative into a positive experience.

The most comfort is gained when we accept ourselves as the person God intended us to be.

A familiar voice comforts the heart.

When you need someone
to comfort you, call upon
a friend.

**Don't allow friendship
to die through your
own negligence.**

Laughter is a wonderful tonic at any time—it can transform even our most unbearable moments.

May all your tears be tears of joy.

Violence begets
violence.

**When the world is covered
in darkness, even the
smallest candle can make
a difference.**

A heart can never
be too full.

Kindness often removes difficulty.

Where there is hatred, there is a path to love.

Where there is injury, there is a path to pardon.

Where there is doubt, there is a path to faith.

Where there is despair, there is a path to hope.

Where there is darkness, there is a path to light.

Where there is sadness, there is a path to joy.

The things that life sends to try us are what character is made from.

No matter how dark things seem to get, there are always possibilities.

Darkness cannot be driven out by darkness.

Hatred cannot be driven out by hatred.

Nothing can
disturb you unless
you allow it to.

Nothing can
frighten you unless
you allow it to.

A comfortable silence is one between two people at ease.

Have patience and, above all, trust in yourself.

What a comfort a dull
but kindly person is,
to be sure, at times!
A ground-glass shade
over a gas-lamp does
not bring more solace
to our dazzled eyes
than such a one to
our minds.

Oliver Wendell Holmes

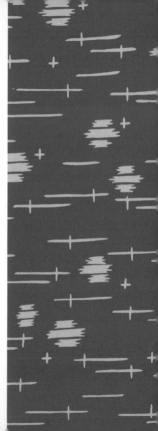

Only when we have full faith in ourselves will we have enough in life.

At those times when things seem bad, there is comfort to be had from knowing things could always have been worse.

When things seem to be at their worst there is comfort to be had from knowing that things can only get better.

The ultimate measure of a man is not where he stands in moments of comfort and convenience, but where he stands at times of challenge and controversy.

Martin Luther King

Suffer nothing to take away your peace.

What I aspired to be and was not, comforts me.

Robert Browning

The only free meal there is in this life is usually attached to a mousetrap.

Before taking comfort in the light at the end of the tunnel, be certain that it is not a train coming straight at you.

If it wasn't for time, everything would happen at once.

Some days it is better by far not to get out of bed.

There are two kinds of people in this world: those who are comforted by others, and those who gain comfort by comforting others.

Most situations are easier to get into than out of.

It is perfectly possible to be ill, poor, or both and still be more comfortable than someone who is rich and healthy.

When you have tried everything else and failed, read the instructions.

We can't help ourselves sometimes. Even when everything seems to be going well we are still compelled to feel that we have overlooked something.

Take no comfort from being informed that something is foolproof. Those who make such claims have little idea just how clever fools actually are.

If you have any doubt, at least make what you say *sound* convincing.

Those who are comfortable applying the laws of logic must also be comfortable in the fact that they might lead to an unexpected conclusion.

There's a difference between being flexible and being indecisive.

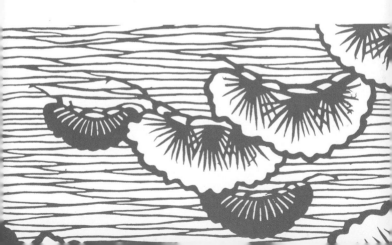

We may not be able to do everything, but we can make sure that we at least do *something*.

A river becomes crooked
because it follows the path
of least resistance.

**Comfort is the journey,
not the destination.**

The best place
to get lost is in
thought.

Keep an open mind about everything.

When you stop at the fountain of knowledge, drink, don't gargle!

**Don't get angry.
Running in circles
shouting and swearing
will solve nothing.**

Enjoy life the way
you want to enjoy it.

**Sometimes the only thing
you can do is pray.**

What the mail man bringeth, the trash man taketh away.

You cannot make a leap in more than one jump.

**Rediscover the importance
of the little things in life.**

Having an idea is
fine, but it requires
you to put it to work.

If you are just testing the water, only put one foot in it.

Nothing is as easy as it looks.

Remember, everything takes longer than you think.

Things will only get worse under pressure.

Very little is truly
as terrible as it
first appears.

We all have ability.
The question is: how
do you use yours?

**He receives comfort like
cold porridge.**

William Shakespeare

Are you ready to take the next thing that comes along?

Be comfortable standing up for an ideal. You're standing on behalf of countless thousands who feel just the way you do.

It doesn't matter what people say or how things turn out when you feel that something makes complete sense at the time. It's called Hope.

Faith and hope are the wings we soar with.

Greed, like the love of comfort, is a kind of fear.

Cyril Connolly

Every experience you have adds to your confidence, adds to your courage.

Was whatever you were worrying about worth losing last night's sleep over?

There's absolutely nothing we can do when our car is stuck in traffic or our flight is overdue. Take the opportunity to relax and take a look at life around you. Then catch up later.

Prosperity is not without many fears and distastes; adversity not without many comforts and hopes.

Francis Bacon

Above all else, know that you have purpose.

Are you comfortable with who you are?

If we were all comfortable just being who we are, we'd only ever have to buy the things we really need and like.

Just because the advertisers consider you to be uncomfortable doesn't mean you have to comply.

Comfort, luxury, and ease are not products to be purchased.

Avoid too much advice offered
to you from a safe harbor.

**He who would pass his declining
years with honor and comfort,
should, when young, consider that
he may one day become old, and
remember when he is old, that he
has once been young.**

Joseph Addison

We all want to live to
a comfortable old age.

Make it your aim to be youthful and alive for the span of your life, and then to die without regrets.

Most of us seem to feel uncomfortable about growing old and remaining youthful in our outlook.

Old age, believe me, is a good and pleasant thing. It is true you are gently shouldered off the stage, but then you are given such a comfortable front stall as spectator.

Jane Harrison

We cannot be made uncomfortable without our approval.

A myth is a useful thing, but there is more comfort in truth.

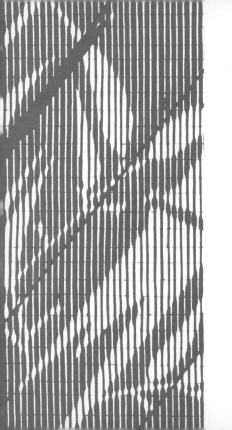

Alcohol and drugs are not providers of comfort. Instead, they momentarily transport us to regions of thought in which we feel we are the master of our destiny.

Take comfort in knowing that without stimulants *you* are the master of your destiny.

Don't become someone else's character type that they will use to comfort themselves.

One person's comfort is another person's gaoler.

For some, a total lack of comfort is pure ecstasy, and when that lack of comfort begins to make them feel comfortable, they feel compelled to move on.

The most comfortable bed is the bed of profound friendship.

There are no comforting words for great bereavement, and no comfort in seeking them. But strangely, there is great comfort to be gained from knowing that we will never be parted from the feeling.

Time is no comforter.

A book will never desert you. It offers good counsel, friendship, comfort, and cheer.

For many, vice is not a road to misery, and virtue will not necessarily lead everyone to happiness.

Except a living man there is nothing more wonderful than a book! A message to us from the dead— from human souls we never saw, who lived, perhaps, thousands of miles away. And yet these, in those little sheets of paper, speak to us, arouse us, terrify us, teach us, comfort us, open their hearts to us as brothers.

Charles Kingsley

Accept your own uniqueness and take comfort in *your* natural environment.

A dancer is comfortable in music.

A reader is
comfortable
in a book.

**A swimmer is
comfortable
in water.**

A lover is
comfortable
in love.

An uncertain guide makes everyone following him uncomfortable.

One can feel safe in comfort but one can learn to love truth.

Even when it is for the better, none of us are completely comfortable with change.

Even if it is from bad to worse, there is a certain relief in change.

As I have often found in traveling in a stagecoach, it is often a comfort to shift one's position, and be bruised in a new place.

Washington Irving

The comfort in having children is far outweighed by the sorrow of parting with them.

Children are not only a great comfort in our old age—they drive us to it.

The lust for comfort, that stealthy thing that enters the house as a guest, and then becomes a host, and then a master.

Kahlil Gibran

All too many in their attempts to comfort those seemingly distressed are blissfully unaware that they are bringing distress to the comfortable.

Of all created comforts, God is the lender; you are the borrower, not the owner.

Samuel Rutherford

There are moments in life when to be scared is sensible, and to be comfortable is suicidal.

Common sense is fine and momentarily comforting, but realize that it can never advance beyond its own limits. True comfort can only come through knowledge.

**Free the spirit of inquiry
that lives within you.**

One person's cheap comfort
is someone else's comfort.

**The pillow will always know just
how comfortable you really are.**

Comfort the afflicted and afflict the constantly complaining comfortable!

I've never any pity for conceited people, because I think they carry their comfort about with them.

George Eliot

Dare and endure—only then will things ease and you will arrive at comfort.

Without comfort within us, external comforts are meaningless.

Keeping Life Manageable

Is it so hard to
live a life that is
manageable?

I'll be old when I feel like it.

Those in doubt
often mumble.

Everything has its reason in life.

The discomfort of taking exercise is nothing compared to the comfort of having taken it.

Those with the most to learn in life are those who feel they know it all.

It is often the case that the people who argue the most are the people who know the least.

Try to please everybody and you will surely fail.

There is no formula for success.

People who walk on thin ice might just as well dance on it.

If you prepare for the future, then the future belongs to you.

Just listen to yourself, then you'll say less about more.

Eat less—but no less than you need.

Instinct is only common sense. With enough instinct anyone can be a genius.

Make your mind up now—how comfortable do you want to be?

When we are prosperous, our friends know us; in adversity, we know our friends.

Everyone needs to assume some responsibility in life.

The reward for doing work
well is being offered the
opportunity to do more.

Charity begins
in the heart.

**Information is helpful, but
if it comes along with
experience it becomes vital.**

You cannot enjoy life if you spend the entire journey fretting about the bumps and potholes.

People who rarely try anything see most things as being impossible.

All the experts you can muster, although united in agreement, can still be mistaken.

Only a fool would be comfortable rejecting wisdom merely for arriving late.

Be prepared to let your standards drop every now and then.

Make love, not paperwork.

Who can be comfortable being cared for by someone who has let their plants die?

We are all of us
nearly angels.

**The level of our comfort
will be determined by the
extent of our belief that we
can be comforted.**

Ability may take you to the top, but it takes character to remain there.

Act as if it were impossible for others to make you feel uncomfortable and it will be so.

Only after you have tried to do your very best will you know if your best was good enough.

Make commitments, not empty promises.

Pity the big fish in a little pond.

Comfort is habit-forming.

What is my attitude
toward comfort?

Bad times have value too.

The most uncommon thing to
discover is common sense.

If we are always busy getting ready to live, when will we find the time to start living?

Don't allow defeat to disappoint you—use it as a stimulus.

Consider the uses of adversity.

Top athletes learn to love their pain and use it positively.

Losers are those who let it happen, winners are those who make it happen.

To do one's best is an awfully big adventure.

Suddenly everything we have prepared for in life meets its opportunity. That is luck.

Principles should never be sacrificed for temporary comforts.

Nothing can stop the person with the right mental attitude.

Nothing can help the person who has the wrong attitude.

Obstacles are rarely seen by those who fix their gaze upon their goal.

If you are uncomfortable about having far to go, how can you ever find out how far you can go?

Those who do only their best work are usually mediocre. Most of us, however, are comfortable knowing that we can always do better.

Comfort is
90% mental.

**There is no greater comfort,
perhaps, than a modest and
healthy level of pride.**

Bad practice does
not make perfect.

When we feel good about ourselves we feel more comfortable about everything—and we produce good results.

Comfort is not the same as rest. Some take their greatest comfort in hard work, some are never more comfortable than when on a long journey.

What sportsperson ever got faster or stronger by doing less?

Do everything with intent, and do not allow yourself to imagine that anything you do is not important.

Be prepared. Comfort requires training and discipline.

Once we experience complete comfort, we seem better prepared to tackle anything in the knowledge that we can return there.

Winners look exactly the same on the outside as losers—the difference is emotional.

For some, when their comfort is on the line, they give their all.

A defeat is only a minor temporary setback.

**One can never be comfortable
while believing that comfort is
beyond their reach.**

One never fails until one quits.

**The bottom of the ladder to
success may be crowded, but there
is always room at the top.**

There are those in life who say
it cannot be done.
And there are those who do it.

**The life we make for ourselves is
proportionate to what we give.**

The desire for comfort may be strong, but just exactly what you are prepared to sacrifice in order to be comfortable is the critical thing.

Have you ever stopped to consider that we all need something in our lives that is the opposite of comfort in order to be comforted?

People find that the harder they work, the luckier they seem to get.

Only when we cross into the foothills of the impossible can we know for certain the limitations of what is possible.

The real test is not avoiding sticky situations, but getting out of a sticky situation once you are in it.

In life, as in everything else, the person who makes the fewest mistakes wins.

There is more ground to be gained from our hopes than from our fears.

The key to doing anything better is to become better at it. We are none of us comfortable about doing something that we are not very good at.

Life tricks us with moments when everything seems to go right, but these soon pass.

We can *want* to do something or we can be *willing* to do something, but whether it gets done or not depends upon us actually *doing* something.

We believe what we fear, and we believe what we desire.

We should fear not living the life we have while we have it rather than go through life fearing the end of life.

How can we ever begin to live while we remain afraid?

Let wonder replace fear.

Fear no one, hate no one.

Hate is the direct
consequence of fear.

**A child who fears noises
grows into an adult who
hates noise.**

There can be no peace where
there is fear.

What are fears but voices airy?
Whispering harm where harm is not.
And deluding the unwary
Till the fatal bolt is shot!

William Wordsworth

On the other side
of fear lies freedom.

**There is a difference
between living a life and
earning a living.**

Good friends, good books,
and a sleepy conscience:
this is the ideal life.

Mark Twain

Living only for comfort is like having a house with many rooms and only ever going into one of them.

Live your life on all its levels:
your physical life
your mental life
your emotional life
and your spiritual life.

I like living. I have sometimes been wildly, despairingly, acutely miserable, racked with sorrow, but through it all I still know quite certainly that just to be alive is a grand thing.

Agatha Christie

When we can find comfort in life we can find comfort in death.

The best cosmetic on offer is joy.

Kindness is produced by kindness.
Cicero

Take care to make your own bed comfortable, for it is you who must lie on it.

Why park your car with an empty fuel tank?

When you see someone that deserves a compliment, why not compliment them?

Some will be comforted by any answer you choose to give them.

Find comfort in who you are.

Find comfort in
what you have.

Find comfort in where you are.

Find comfort in
who you are with.

Take comfort from your decisions.

Take comfort from your actions.

Take comfort from your choices.

**Our families and
our friends make
our house a home.**

A friend is a
family member
that we have
been able to
choose.

**All good things
are yours.**

While you are waiting,
life is passing you by.

**Within reason, do the
things you want to.**

Fear less, love more.

It takes your consent for anyone to be able to make you feel inferior.

Don't stray from the path.

By taking the first things first even the most complex of human problems can be reduced to a manageable proportion.

The only completely stress-free environment is the grave.

Start seeing stress as a challenge, not a threat.

The right to mismanage your own affairs is known as freedom.

Contrary to popular belief, things refuse to be mismanaged for long.

When we manage to make ourselves understood, it's a good sign that we are speaking well.

Do you think with your head or your heart?

Attitude is contagious.
Those who are
comfortable with
themselves give a
comforting aura to all
those around them.

Small is
Beautiful

There is no situation that doesn't look better after singing under the shower.

Great things are not done by impulse, but by a series of small things brought together.

Vincent van Gogh

Go out looking for comfort and it will elude you. Comfort starts with the mind.

A comfortable life is about not being affected by the flow but living despite it, like a riverbed rock, anchored by your principles.

Comfort begins when we can begin to treat others in the way we would like them to treat us.

When was the last time you shut yourself off from everything else and watched the sun set?

When was the last time you shut yourself off from everything else and watched the sun rise?

When was the last time you shut yourself off from everything else and listened to the rain fall? A child laugh? A bird sing?

183

One person's comfort is another person's discomfort.

Like leaving the toilet seat up, or hanging pantyhose up to dry.

Sometimes there is more comfort to be gained by baking and enjoying a good cake or loaf of bread than by traveling five thousand miles in search of a beach.

We get close when we strive for excellence, not for perfection.

Plant a rose or, better still, a tree in honor of your birthday.

Why go through a lifetime of discomfort caused by not telling someone that you love them?

Never waste an opportunity to say exactly what you mean.

Never waste an opportunity to say exactly how you feel.

There are some amongst us on this earth who manage to leave everything a little better than it was before.

Life…
Keep it simple.

**Think big thoughts while
relishing small pleasures.**

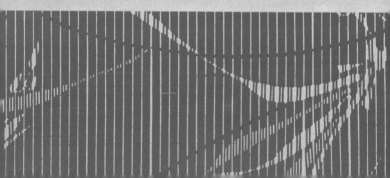

If the most positive and enthusiastic person you know is not yourself, then something needs adjusting.

None of us savors the moment that the hygienist suggests we should floss our teeth. There is double comfort to be gained from beating him to it.

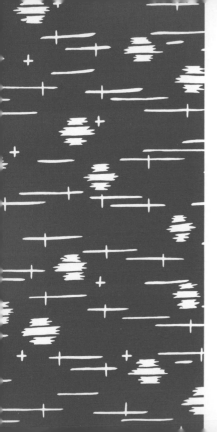

There is less
discomfort
in asking for
a raise when
you believe
that you
have earned
it than in
bottling up
resentment
inside you.

If you want to feel exceptionally good, overtip a waitress.

You will not find comfort if you are incapable of forgiving yourself and others.

When did you last hear yourself saying "Thank you?"

When was the last time you heard yourself say "Please?"

Often the most precious moments in life are made by the simplest things, like buying a glass of lemonade.

Try polishing your shoes.

Avoid negative
people at all costs.

**Whose birthday did you
forget today?**

**Improving yourself is a lifetime commitment.
Are you worth it?**

Some are comfortable in the knowledge that they have a spare tire in their car.

Nobody who goes to bed armed to the teeth can be comfortable.

Tell others how wonderful you think they are.

Tell yourself, "This is my life and I won't let anyone bring fear into it."

Never be afraid to look people in the eye.

Never be too shy to be the first to say hello.

If you lock your best china cups away for special occasions, you may never get to use them.

If you must borrow anything, return it the moment you have finished with it.

Always make room in your life for new friends, but cherish the old ones.

Many of us go through life burdened by secrets.

Do not shy
away from an
outstretched hand.

Sing more.

**There is little comfort
to be gained from
blaming others.**

Keep a pet.

We must each be prepared to take responsibility for every area of our life.

A wave thrown is like a kiss blown.

Will you be there when people need you?

Have you ever seen the expression on the face of a traffic warden when you feed a stranger's expired meter?

You will
never find
comfort
while you
expect
life to be
fair.

Who can estimate the power of love?

Comfort does not lie in the bottom of a glass.

There is little point to a life that must be constantly explained. Take comfort in who you are.

We should never be afraid to admit that we have made a mistake.

When you don't know something, admit it. What is more unnerving than saying you know something when you don't?

Even small improvements deserve compliments.

Never let anything interfere with keeping a promise, but make sure that you can keep a promise before you make it.

A softer sofa might take up more space.

If at all, marry for love.

Rekindling old friendships is rejuvenating.

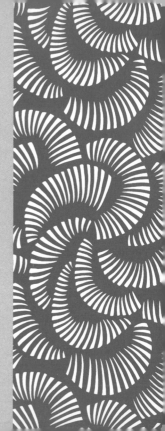

Once you start counting your blessings it may be hard to stop.

Waiting at the other end of the telephone line is someone who wants to hear from you.

We all have it within us to be a success—it has nothing to do with what we have or where we have come from.

Even very successful people make mistakes. Perhaps what stands them apart from many of us is that they are careful not to repeat them.

If you are frightened of making mistakes, you will never attempt anything.

An entire lifetime can be wasted going the wrong way about something. Always open your ears to the advice of others.

If you go through life playing by the rules, you must be prepared to rewrite them along the way.

Be comfortable in asking for help.

No one person becomes successful without the help of others.

Try to leave time to hear the birds sing the dawn chorus at least once a year.

Luck plays no part in making a success out of life. We are life, and life is what we make of it.

Work hard, be diligent, acquire knowledge, and apply yourself.

Money is no measure of a successful life.

Sometimes we are successful and are the only ones who know it.

Ask yourself, "What is my vision for the future?" It need not be great, but it is important that you have one.

Ask yourself, "What is my mission in life?" It needn't be mammoth in order to benefit mankind.

Ask yourself, "What is the purpose of my life?" Even if we feel we exist just to keep the balance of nature, we are all vital in the infinite scheme of things.

A comfortable life is achieved when we can reach a balance between life and work.

Even those we consider successful have their ups and downs.

Try if you can to manage time better. It is the one thing that can never be replaced.

Anything that we simply tolerate in our life is a cause of discomfort.

Never fear failure.
It is part of life's pattern.

It takes great courage, wisdom, and self-determination to know when to quit.

Setting goals
does not guarantee
achieving them.

**Age is not half as important
as attitude.**

I intend never to feel
as old as I am.

Those of us with poor memory are able to experience things for the very first time over and over again.

The age we feel in our heart is often misrepresented by the hair on our head.

Those who are broad-minded can see both sides of the coin.

To someone celebrating their 100th birthday, anyone under the age of 90 is young.

Comfort is snuggling down with a hot water bottle on a cold winter night.

Whatever your reflection tells you, the spirit does not grow old.

Rule your mind, or let your mind rule you.

It doesn't matter if it's a church or a bicycle shop, when you love somebody you tell them so anywhere.

If you want to look good, wear a smile.

Most people would succeed in small things if they were not troubled with great ambitions.
Henry Wadsworth Longfellow

Most of the trouble we have in our lives never actually happens.

Life is
how you
make it.

Almost everybody is good at heart.

Everything improves with laughter.

Wrinkles can be comfortable to those with old memories and youthful thoughts.

Keep away from small people who try to belittle your ambitions. Small people always do that, but the really great make you feel that you, too, can become great.

Mark Twain

We pray for a long life, and yet we fear old age.

An improved attitude leads to an improved memory.

For the ignorant, old age is as winter; for the learned, it is the harvest.

Few people know how to be old.

Old age should be worn with pride. There are many to whom it is denied.

The length of a film should be directly related to the endurance of the human bladder.

Alfred Hitchcock

If you can't find comfort in your own garden, what makes you feel you'll be able to find it anywhere else?

Reflected in the eyes of a child
are the flames of youth.
And in the eyes of the elderly
is the light of experience.

**One person's itch is
another person's allergy.**

Laugh and the world laughs with you; snore and you sleep alone.

Anthony Burgess

Think happy thoughts, find new interests, and take some outdoor exercise.

Do you suppose we grow older because we stop playing?

At this precise moment, there are countless thousands discovering the ways not to do something.

From small beginnings come great things.

If your strength is small, don't carry heavy burdens. If your words are worthless, don't give advice.

To a three-year-old the greatest toy is a worm.

Put your heart, mind, intellect, and soul even to your smallest acts. This is the secret of success.

Sri Swami Sivananda

Even the smallest good deed is better than the grandest intention.

Everything is merely the sum of its parts.

You can do small things in a great way.

They say that the best things come in small packages.

By depending on the great, the small may rise high. See, the little plant ascending the tall tree has climbed to the top.

Saskya Pandita

No act of kindness,
no matter how small,
is ever wasted.

Aesop

**What if a coincidence is
actually a small miracle in
which God has chosen to
remain anonymous?**

Friends and Family

Treat your family like friends and your friends like family.

The curious thing about families is that they allow you to become intimately acquainted with people you might never have even introduced yourself to.

The most sacred group is a loving family.

A family is a little kingdom, torn with factions and exposed to revolutions.

Samuel Johnson

The family—nature's masterpiece.

I have found the best way to give advice
to your children is to find out what they
want and then advise them to do it.

Harry S. Truman

Children teach us what life is all about.

To show a child what once delighted
you, to find the child's delight added to
your own. This is happiness.

J.B. Priestley

By the time we come to realize that our parents were right, we usually have children of our own who think we are wrong.

What children need more than anything else is your time.

Children produce adults.

A good friend is rather like a well-made quilt—well-crafted, complex, comfortable to have around, to be valued forever, and always willing to offer warmth.

Friends are like flowers—once planted they can make our life a garden.

Express yourself.

If you've still got any real friends left when your time comes to die, then you will have had a wonderful life.

Life is just a matter of time.

Be he a king or a peasant, he is happiest who finds peace at home.
  Johann Wolfgang von Goethe

Begin each day with love in your heart.

Begin each day with calm nerves.

Begin each day with truth in your mind.

Begin each day with
peace in your sights.

Begin each day with
a sense of wonder.

Begin each day
willing to learn.

A man can't make a place for himself in the sun if he keeps taking refuge under the family tree.

Helen Keller

Family love is messy, clinging, and of an annoying and repetitive pattern, like bad wallpaper.

Friedrich Nietzsche

Every human being, regardless of religion, culture, color, and creed, is a member of humanity and the human family.

Some families should certainly not keep parrots as pets.

Even if you're on the right track,
you'll get run over if you just sit there.

When you are investigating the unknown, how do you know when you have found it?

No matter how small, do something special today, and every day, for your loved one.

In any relationship it's the little things that count.

To put the world in order, we must first put the nation in order; to put the nation in order, we must put the family in order; to put the family in order, we must cultivate our personal life; and to cultivate our personal life, we must first set our hearts right.

Confucius

Make the most of everyday things en route to your bigger life goals.

Dreams and aspirations are fine to have, but they are not enough without someone in your life to share them with.

The family is the association established by nature for the supply of man's everyday wants.

Aristotle

Without comfort a thousand books are not enough and one word is too much.

Where there is great doubt, there will be a great awakening.

Where there is small doubt, there will be a small awakening.

Where there is no doubt, there will be no awakening.

Despite everything, mountains are mountains, waters are waters.

Even if we do nothing at all, the spring arrives and the grass grows.

A coin is only worth something when you let it slip from your grasp.

When you understand, then things are just as they are.

When you do not understand, then things are just as they are.

Everything is just as it is.

Be like a child. For them, every moment and every thing is brand new.

Sometimes the obstacle we must overcome is the path itself.

If we can concentrate on our everyday routine we will be on the Zen path.

Don't worry about catching cold when you have just been saved from drowning.

Love is the music
that brings harmony.

Love is the oil that
eases friction.

Love is the cement
that binds.

Worry is more exhausting than running a marathon.

As a cure for worrying, work is better than whiskey.
Ralph Waldo Emerson

You will not defeat tomorrow's difficulties by worrying, you will only serve to drain today of its strength.

Ask yourself: How important is it?

Turn your worries into concerns; that way, instead of worrying about problems you can concern yourself with solving them.

Difficult times have helped me to understand better than before, how infinitely rich and beautiful life is in every way, and that so many things that one goes worrying about are of no importance whatsoever.

Isak Dinesen

Chances are that the things we haven't worried about are the things that will happen.

Reality does not age us half as swiftly as apprehension.

It is the anticipation that creates the terror.

When the sun is not shining and the rain is not falling, only worriers put up their umbrellas.

Worry will give even the smallest thing a big shadow.

Goodness, mercy, and kindness are three little words that the comfort of the entire human race depend upon.

Use all obstacles as stepping stones in order to build the life you want.

Show me a person unable to make decisions and I will show you someone who doesn't know their own values.

Live your life from your heart.

Share with others from your heart.

Any belief worth having must survive doubt.

Doubt is not a pleasant condition, but certainty is absurd.

Voltaire

People tend only to see the deed and not the motive behind it.

The grandest intention is worth nothing without action.

Our deeds determine us.

What we have been helps to make us what we are.

Be good.
Do good.
Feel good.

To be complete, your compassion must include yourself.

For every human being who cries out to us for help, there are perhaps a million or so others in the world who are equally entitled to attention.

If we are to expect our children to give comfort to others, then we must allow them to come to know comfort first within their own family.

Stop and realize—we are all part of one another, and all involved in one another.

Compassion means there can never really be any peace and joy for those who care about you until there is peace and joy for you.

Compassion is the basis
of morality.

Arnold Schopenhauer

**If you want others to be happy,
practice compassion. If you want to
be happy, practice compassion.**

The Dalai Lama

The dew of compassion
is a tear.

Lord Byron

There can be no person alive who doesn't appreciate kindness and compassion.

It is the easiest thing in the world to criticize.

There are none so certain as those that misunderstand the question.

For comfort's sake, never bathe too long in the sunshine of people's opinion.

No thought worth thinking should be uncomfortable.

Tear yourself away from the safe comfort of certainties. Learn to love truth, and truth will reward you.

Does anyone honestly do anything more in life than seek to secure for themselves peace of mind and spiritual comfort?

We must always weigh our material comforts against our moral growth.

Most of the luxuries and many of the
so-called comforts of life are not only
not indispensable, but positive
hindrances to the elevation of mankind.

Henry David Thoreau

**A friend is someone we can feel
safe with.**

Who can be comfortable and well-fed,
while all around people are starving?

**A huge fortune does not necessarily
contribute to great beauty.**

When men are easy in their circumstances, they are naturally enemies to innovations.

Joseph Addison

Many a lifetime is wasted away by those too preoccupied with their search for ways to make their life even more comfortable.

The ultimate measure of a person is not where that person stands at moments of comfort.

Will anyone's being comfortable enrich the world?

When we are thrown in at the deep end, we are faced with this choice: sink or swim.

Every day there is the chance to learn something new.

The bees know that the farmer who wants a healthy crop always helps his poorer neighbor out with good seed.

Luxury and comfort are not our main requirements in life.

Where there is enthusiasm to be found, happiness awaits.

Sometimes the greatest comfort comes when we can be genuinely happy over someone else's good fortune.

Ask this: What am I doing for others?

The path of selfishness is dark and destructive.

You can feel safe that a true friend will make certain that when you open your mouth your brains don't spill out.

Ignorance won't kill you, but it can make you sweat at times.

Many a time, from a bad beginning, a great friendship has sprung up.

Imagine the very best friend a person could ever have, and then become that friend yourself to someone in your life.

Don't wait for people to be friendly. Show them how it's done.

Care about the values your friend holds and your friend will care about yours.

A friend is someone who will sit with you on cold winter nights and walk with you in silence.

**Be comforted in the knowledge
that you have a friend who
won't let you down.**

A friend walks in when the rest
of the world walks out on you.

**A friend is someone who shares
your sense of joy and humor.**

A good friend is there when life demands more strength than you alone can muster.

A friend is someone who looks forward to the times you are together.

A friend looks beyond your failures. Share your point of view.

Take the trouble to tell someone just how much their friendship means.

What friendship can cross our path and leave no trace?

A friend is someone who believes in you, despite evidence to the contrary.

What friend would not rather hear of your love now than have it carved on their tombstone later?

Be slow to fall into friendship; but when thou art in, continue firm and constant.

Socrates

If only we could feel comfortable saying the kind of things we mean to say when those we love are gone, before they go.

Good Food/ Good Health

There is a saying around the globe that laughter is brightest where the food is best.

Love well.
Sleep well.
Dine well.
Think well.

Who cannot feel benevolent following a good meal?

When people discover they have managed to live to a ripe old age, they soon realize they should have taken better care of themselves.

My doctor told me to stop having intimate dinners for four. Unless there are three other people.

Orson Welles

When planning a menu, consider whether you wish to leave your guests overjoyed or hope to never see them again.

After a good dinner one can forgive anybody, even one's own relatives.

Oscar Wilde

Comfort is a neatly arranged, well-provisioned breakfast-table.

Food is
the gateway
that can
lead us
directly to
our past.

Eat less fat and eat less sugar.

Seek comfort in grains, cereals, and pulses.

We are what we eat.

Each of us has our own doctor within us.

I know the look of an apple that is roasting and sizzling on the hearth on a winter's evening, and I know the comfort that comes of eating it hot, along with some sugar and a drench of cream…I know how the nuts taken in conjunction with winter apples, cider, and doughnuts, make old people's tales and old jokes sound fresh and crisp and enchanting.

Mark Twain

Who can comfort better
than a chef?

**There is little that cannot be
achieved when one has a bowl
of pistachio nuts.**

Soup not only warms you and
is easy to swallow and to
digest, it also creates the
illusion that Mother is there.

Marlene Dietrich

That which is great is constructed by adding little to a little for as long as it takes.

When we understand that there is nothing that is too little for man, then we can work at having little misery in our lives, thus leaving more room for happiness.

There are some who, from time to time, put on great shows of their talents. But people are more comfortable with those who regularly perform small kindnesses or willingly show us a little consideration.

There is no little thing that is not of consequence. Even the tiniest thing can have monumental consequences.

When we are comfortable taking on a little at a time, there is nothing that can't be done.

Be true to your teeth, or your teeth will be false.

If you want to send someone you care for a warming present, make it thermal socks.

A cheerful face is nearly as good for an invalid as healthy weather.

Benjamin Franklin

Age isn't a question of years, it is about temperament and health. Some are born old, while others never grow up.

Just because we're no longer children doesn't mean we stop growing.

It is not good for all our wishes to be fulfilled. Through sickness we recognize the value of health; through evil, the value of good; through hunger, the value of food; through exertion, the value of rest.

It's not what happens to you, but how you react to it that matters.

Epictetus

Those who have discovered serenity before us have described it not as being free from the storms but finding peace within them.

Man needs difficulties; they are necessary for health.

Carl Jung

To do the big things in life we should not put our trust in those people who can't be bothered with the little things.

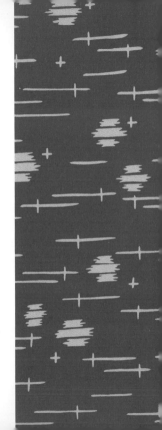

Try to curry favor
with everybody.

**A good soup is as
comforting as a
good pillow.**

Give yourself a reward system
for the things you have done.

Only through in-depth study of what at first sight appears to be insignificant do we really learn a great deal.

Those amongst us who are the happiest are not those who experience one major piece of good fortune but those who discover something little to their advantage every day.

A good meal soothes the soul.

Can anything evoke feelings of innocent delight in us like the smell of baking bread?

What does cookery mean? It means the knowledge of Medea and of Circe, and of Calypso, and Sheba. It means knowledge of all herbs, and fruits, and balms and spices… It means the economy of your great-grandmother and the science of modern chemistry, and French art, and Arabian hospitality. It means, in fine, that you are to see imperatively that everyone has something nice to eat.

John Ruskin

Some of the greatest symphonies have been composed on the cooker.

Strange to see how a good dinner and feasting reconciles everybody.
Samuel Pepys

Food can only be brought to life if you love it enough. Comfort food comes from the heart.

If it makes you feel more comfortable start your meal by eating dessert.

No composer will play his music exactly the same each time. Instead he will interpret it anew for each performance. The same should be said for a recipe.

Trust your palate and your instinct and you will soon become comfortable with your culinary abilities.

The moment you feel comfortable around food and its preparation, you can lock the cookbooks away in your archive.

Some prefer the comfort of knowing the cow and the chicken provided breakfast, not some scientist.

When asked if they liked chocolate, 90% of people said they did, and the other 10% said they did also.

A good meal regenerates the body.

Eating is believing.

One of the most direct routes to a person's comfort zone is via ice cream.

If more of us valued food
and cheer and song
above hoarded gold, it
would be a merrier world.

J. R. R. Tolkien

Many a crisis has been resolved over a five-course dinner.

Comfort: a warm room, a cosy sofa, soothing music, and a sauce simmering in the kitchen.

Get the people eating and the anger will subside.

Every cake
has a soul.

**Never be frantic, angry,
or rushed.**

An act of creativity is an act
of integrity.

We can all be creative when
we cook.

The most important ingredient in comfort food is the spirit you put into it.

Wars could be resolved if the weapons were taken away and people threw excellent chocolates at each other instead.

Chocolate has few enemies.

Just because something promises to be nourishing, doesn't mean we will all feel comfortable eating it.

A heavy loaf is not necessarily a good loaf.

The best place to practice self-expression is in the kitchen through your cooking.

The greatest national philosophy is to be discovered in any nation's diet.

The art of dining well is no slight art, the pleasure not a slight pleasure.

Michel de Montaigne

Food is a necessity and should be available to all.

It is hard to take comfort in food when so many have none at all.

If comfort comes in the form of food, then comfort will only go to those with the money to buy.

Save your modesty for God, but show the world you are pleased with what you have done.

If you have enthusiasm, you must learn to feel comfortable about showing it.

Of soup and love, the first is best.

Spanish proverb

The most primitive form of comfort, and has been for thousands of years, is, of course, food.

Who can be comfortable knowing they have never tried to overcome their fear of cookery?

The discovery of a new dish does more for the happiness of the human race than the discovery of a star.

Anthelme Brillat-Savarin

To cook really well one must love, and have respect for, food.

Take comfort in the preparation of good food.

When you feel you
are alone, it is time
to eat garlic.

Prepare something delicious
and present it with ceremony.

**Life is only as delicious
as we make it.**

Snuggle up with a slice
of homebaked pie.

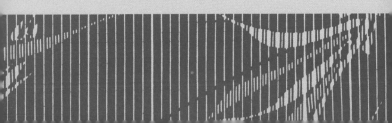

The closest we can get to artificially creating a daydream is a well-prepared dessert.

Life is made up of small pleasures.

Happiness is made up of those tiny successes.

Centimeters and milliseconds make champions.

Do little things with great love. That way all that you do will be great.

If you want
to achieve
a healthy
outlook, get
a smile.

Life, from generation to generation, is like recycling.

Each generation must pick out what is good and useful to them where they can find it.

Triumph in
little things—
triumph in life.

Some will go through life accepting it for what it is, and others will only ever accept it as it is not.

If we were to succumb to an eye-for-an-eye approach to life, most people in this world would be blind.

A little time put aside for special things soon adds up. If everybody put aside ten minutes a day, everybody could read the entire Bible this year.

May the breath of kindness blow everything else away.

Just because we might have become accustomed to being harmed a little on a regular basis by our conditions or circumstances does not mean we are comfortable with the situation.

Do not assume that she who seeks to comfort you now, lives untroubled among the simple and quiet words that sometimes do you good. Her life may also have much sadness and difficulty, that remains far beyond yours. Were it otherwise, she would never have been able to find these words.

Rainer Maria Rilke

When you reach that moment will you, can you, say:

I am comfortable being old.

I am comfortable with my color…
I am comfortable being with people
who are not my color.

**I am comfortable with my weight…
I am comfortable being with people
who are not my weight.**

I am comfortable with my height…
I am comfortable being with people
who are not my height.

**I am comfortable with my age…
I am comfortable being with people
who are not my age.**

I am not comfortable in the company of
those who are comfortable in the
presence of danger.

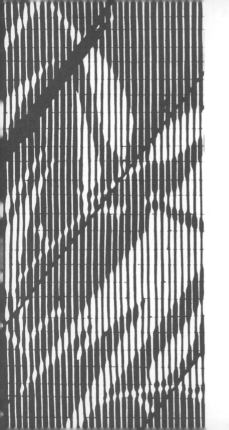

The weak never stop to think that there is another way.

There is character in resolve.

Strength is about recognizing that change is needed and working towards making that change, regardless of how difficult or unlikely it may seem.

The way to overcome great problems or obstacles is to start immediately, by doing all the small things you make your mind up to do, no matter how much you don't want to do them right now.

Today, open your eyes for the very first time. What do you see?

Ambition requires knowledge.

The fountain of youth is within us all, but it only gets turned on when we do the things we enjoy.

Begin at once to live, and count each separate day as a separate life.

Seneca

By three methods we may learn wisdom:
First, by reflection, which is noblest;
Second, by imitation, which is easiest;
Third, by experience, which is the bitterest.

Confucius

Life will persist until the moment we give up.

The world is full of talented, unsuccessful people, unsung heroes, unrewarded geniuses, educated failures, and myself.

Let enthusiasm work its wonders for you.

Persistence and determination alone are omnipotent.

Calvin Coolidge

To accomplish great things, we must not only act, but also dream; not only plan, but also believe.

Anatole France

Accept the challenges life throws at you. That way you will learn to know your strengths.

We are always rich when we can find comfort in our life.

It takes just as much effort to lose as it does to win.

Character is what you really are; your reputation is only what others think you are.

Destiny is a matter of choice, a thing to be achieved.

Why live anything other than the life you dream of living?

Nothing in life is to be feared. It is only to be understood.

Marie Curie

I don't want to be dying up until the moment that I am no longer alive. I want to live right up to the moment that I die.

And in the end, it's not the years in your life that count. It's the life in your years.

Abraham Lincoln

I feel the end approaching.
Quick, bring me my dessert,
coffee, and liqueur.

attributed to Anthelme Brillat-Savarin's
great aunt Pierette

Being with Others

The willingness to share what you have is more important than what you have.

There is no delight in owning anything unshared.

Seneca

A friend can turn a lemon into lemonade.

Friendship is the only guarantee of peace.

The wonderful thing about having a close friend is that your joys can be doubled and your troubles halved.

Can you be comfortable with anyone who wishes you well for their sake not yours?

Would you be comfortable to honor a friend who has prospered and not feel envy?

No true friend can, or would want, to have power over you.

In a friend we seek someone who is more than just a reflection of ourselves and who acts just as we act.

Friendship is tested to breaking point where there is a reward at stake.

We cannot all choose to live with the best but we can certainly choose not to live with the worst.

No new relationship can be forged without appreciation.

Friendship is like an exotic fruit: delicious to taste but slow to mature and ripen.

Be thankful for those people who are able to rekindle your inner spirit.

The only cure for hatred is friendship.

Cross a friend and you will gain a bitter enemy.

Only the young
know everything.

**A true friend is one
soul in two bodies.**
                    Aristotle

We live at a time when the
strongest nations of the world
have become united by a
common hatred, not respect.

It is much easier to be critical than to be correct.

Benjamin Disraeli

Man will occasionally stumble over the truth…but most of the time he just stumbles.

If you're able to keep your head when all about you are losing theirs, then to many it will appear that you don't understand the gravity of the situation.

You yourself, as much as anybody in the entire universe, deserve your love and affection.

Buddha

Fill someone's life with sweetness.

A cheering word will always find a welcoming ear.

No person we care about can be made to feel too happy.

Hearts are made to be thrilled.

…if at the end, when I come to lay
down the reins of power, I have lost
every other friend on earth, I shall at
least have one friend left, and that
friend shall be down inside of me.

Abraham Lincoln

You can search throughout the entire universe for someone who is more deserving of your love and affection than you are yourself, and that person is not to be found anywhere.

Don't misunderstand true friendship by expecting it to be serene.

A good friend will never have to check the calendar to make time for you in their life.

Each friend represents a world in us, a world possibly not born until they arrive, and it is only by this meeting that a new world is born.

Anaïs Nin

A true friend will always be there for you, even when they'd prefer to be anywhere else.

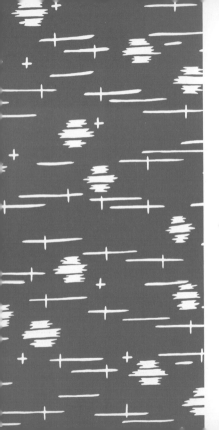

The
purpose
of life is
to live it.

**If you really
want to know
your faults,
confide in a
true friend.**

Take comfort in the fact that you can do anything until you choose to prove to yourself that you can't.

Go oft to the house of thy friend, for weeds choke the unused path.

Ralph Waldo Emerson

Take comfort in the fact that everything that causes you fear is an experience that will strengthen your life.

Why fear new experiences?

It hurts when we fail, but it hurts even more when we know we never even tried to succeed.

In life we get nothing without some effort.

The only thing to fear is fear.

Terror paralyzes our efforts
to progress.

**Even death is not to be feared
by one who has lived wisely.**

Buddha

When you can live and not fear
truth, then you will never have
to live in fear of lies.

Share a little of what you are good at doing.

Be comfortable with nature— nature is a friend to truth.

A single candle can light many others; so it is with happiness and people.

Two people exchanging their ideas will each go away with two ideas.

Is there anything better than mankind's ability to share his feelings and thoughts through language?

What better form of sharing than two friends bringing out the best in each other?

The meeting of two personalities is like the contact of two chemical substances; if there is any reaction, both are transformed.

Carl Jung

It is the things we have in common that make relationships enjoyable.

If you can disagree and still hold hands, you will share good times.

It is the little differences between us that make us interesting.

The pursuit, even of the best things, ought to be calm and tranquil.

Cicero

There is the enchantment of mystery to look forward to in every pursuit.

No act of kindness should be considered small.

Kindness always feels good, whether we are receiving it or offering it to others.

He that does good to another does good also to himself.

Seneca

We know a tree by its fruit and we know a person by their deeds.

When we are happy with someone, we doubt nothing. But when we are unhappy together, we tend to doubt everything.

Sow courtesy.
Reap friendship.

Plant kindness.
Harvest love.

**Before complaining about how
you are regarded by others, you
should reflect upon how you have
contributed to their happiness.**

In human relationships,
kindness and lies are worth
a thousand truths.

Graham Greene

**In truth, we love others not
for who they are, but for
how they make us feel.**

Do not enter into a relationship looking for what you can get out of it, but rather what you can put into it.

Our relationships with others begin to decay when we insist upon analyzing them too closely.

There is no dignity to relationships that are based on obligation.

The quality of our life can be assessed by the quality of our relationships.

When we do things in the spirit of friendship or the spirit of love, at those moments we are truly alive.

Does the object you now have retain the same qualities it had when it was something you desired?

Do not pursue property and position at the expense of your nerves.

I celebrate myself, and sing myself.
Walt Whitman

Never cease in your pursuit of your individuality.

Never be afraid to praise and celebrate your life.

Don't live your life afraid of misfortune.

One word left unsaid during a lifetime will become a stream of tears by the graveside.

Make every day a celebration of living.

Celebrate life's journey all the way, and no road will ever be too rocky.

Good times gallop into our lives like wild horses. Ride them as ecstatically as you wish, but don't hurt yourself when they throw you.

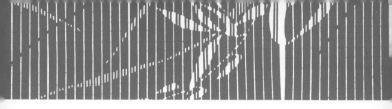

Learn to love your life. It is the only one you will get.

A good night's sleep is always regarded as being ten minutes longer than the one we've had.

Try always to have something to look forward to waking up for.

Have and show enthusiasm.

Don't be put off
by complication.

Avoid disillusionment.

Provide truth and
demand truth.

Take care—you may be compelled to become what you pretend to be.

The only way to have a friend is to be one.
Ralph Waldo Emerson

When someone knows all about you and likes you anyway, that is friendship.

If you only had the energy in you for one last smile in this life, who would you give it to?

When you are able to transplant your enthusiasm into the hearts of others, it is called charisma.

Be tender with the young—
for we are all young sometime.

**Be compassionate with the
aged—for we are all aged
sometime.**

Be sympathetic with those
who strive—for we all strive for
something.

Beware of dedicating yourself to anyone who is not prepared to question their own principles.

Whether it's with family or friends, who can flourish in an atmosphere where individual differences are not appreciated, mistakes are not tolerated, where there is little or no communication, and rules are totally inflexible?

Respect and joy in each other's lives—those are the secrets of family life and friendship.

Those who are free of resentful thoughts surely find peace.

Buddha

For your own sake, learn to forgive those who have offended you.

A wise man will make haste to forgive, because he knows the true value of time, and will not suffer it to pass away in unnecessary pain.

Samuel Johnson

To be wronged is nothing unless you choose to continue to remember it.

When we are comfortable with ourselves, the more likely we will be to treat others with respect, kindness, and generosity.

Sometimes your smile is precisely what someone else needs.

Happiness for an hour can be gained by lying in the sun. Happiness for a day can be achieved by swimming in the sea. Happiness for a year can come with a windfall.

But happiness for a lifetime can only be found by helping somebody else.

One does nothing who tries to console a despondent person with word. A friend is one who aids with deeds at a critical time when deeds are called for.

Plautus

The sun at home always warms better than it does anywhere else.

A heart well prepared for adversity in bad times hopes, and in good times fears for a change in fortune.

Horace

Adversity often draws people together and curiously, more often than not, produces greater harmony in life's relationships.

Friendship doubles our joy and divides our grief.

Leave the moment behind, but never forget what it has taught you.

**The peculiar thing about tragedy
is that it provides one with the
drive to say the things that would
otherwise be left unsaid.**

The true end of tragedy is
to purify the passions.

Aristotle

The curious thing about people is that the moment they are free to do exactly as they please, they imitate each other.

Next time you stare up into the starlit sky and wonder if there is intelligent life in space, you might as well ask if there is intelligent life on earth.

The trouble with the world is that the stupid are cocksure and the intelligent are full of doubt.

Bertrand Russell

There are good things in this life that we will only ever come to know through tragedy.

There is nothing assured to mortals.

Horace

Who on earth would be comfortable having everybody like them? We each have some people we would rather not want to have liking us.

Those who go through life thinking themselves better are not comfortable with others or with themselves.

Say, "I am comfortable being me."

Dwell upon your strengths and you will soon gain confidence.

Comfort is not concerning ourselves about our status in the estimation of others.

Know this—there is no greater impediment to being on good terms with others than being ill at ease with yourself.

Embrace
Life

Heaven can be enjoyed here and now on earth, while we are alive.

If you work hard then you can rest hard in comfort.

There is no substitute for the effort and hard work we put into life.

These are what strengthen us, shape our character, and satisfy the soul.

Life is either a series of trials or challenges, depending on your frame of mind.

When we do not allow ourselves to be mentally defeated, we can never fail.

Too many of us never try because we fear that we might fail.

Determined people outlast the tough times.

We must keep what we hope to accomplish weighed in proportion to the effort we put into our attempt.

Anyone can be successful if they choose to do those things that life's failures refuse to do.

What lies behind us and ahead of us matters not compared to that which lies within us.

You may think you can or you might think you can't. Either way, you are right.

Ask yourself what is the point in striving for mediocrity?

Be yourself, be happy with yourself. That is the foundation of success.

Trying to win is everything. Winning isn't.

Make goals for yourself, not excuses.

We have the choice between solving our problems or being defeated by them.

**Leave nothing undone
which is better done.**

Do nothing that is
better left undone.

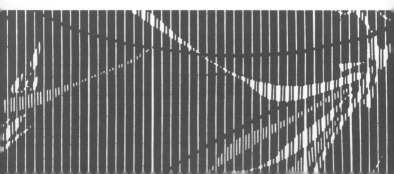

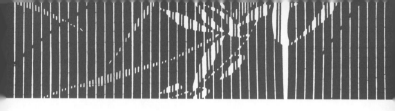

Each day see improvement in yourself.

Try and do things right all the time—this is the secret of winning.

Winning can become a habit, and so too can losing.

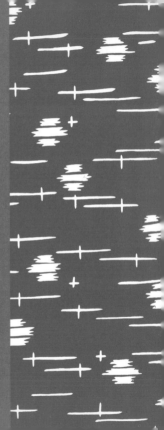

Winners make things happen—losers let things happen.

Whether we win or lose, that we played at all was a winning decision.

The only lasting motivation is self-motivation.

Wishes take a lot of work to make come true.

Spend your day wisely.

You can do your best, but you can always do better.

You can't do anything if you're busy doing nothing.

Each of us creates
our own luck.

**We only become good at
what we practice.**

There is an experience in
taking part that goes beyond
just winning.

The
toughest
opponent
that we will
ever have
to face is
the one
that stares
back at us
from the
mirror.

Spend life searching for the meaning of happiness and you will never be happy.

Spend life searching for the meaning of life and you will never live.

One person's world is another planet's hell.

Every living person has creative potential: we all must create ourselves.

You will never find yourself by looking beyond yourself.

Seize the moment—
every moment.

Life is just one great big opportunity.

We all have strengths, we all have weaknesses.

We don't believe in something simply because we have heard it.

We don't believe in something just because it is spoken about by many.

We don't believe in something purely because it is written somewhere.

We don't believe in traditions because they have been handed down over the generations.

Our teachers and our elders are not always absolutely right. They are our guides.

Do not be too timid and squeamish about your actions. All life is an experiment. The more experiments you make the better. What if they are a little coarse and you may get your coat soiled or torn? What if you do fail and get fairly rolled in the dirt once or twice? Up again; you shall never be so afraid of a tumble.

Ralph Waldo Emerson

Anything that agrees with reason is conducive to good, will benefit one and all, and is something to live up to.

All there is of ourselves is ourself, and it is up to each of us to make the most of ourself.

Who can bring us peace and comfort if not ourselves?

If we can each day conquer one fear, our life will become more comfortable by the day.

Many a life has been wasted shackled to security.

If I cannot win, then at least let me be brave in the attempt.

Our mental attitude makes our world what it is for each of us. Heaven on earth or a living hell—we must choose.

We must not become the victims of our own free will.

The whole world is in our own minds.

Our thoughts make things beautiful, just as our thoughts make things ugly.

Learn to see things in the proper light.

There is meaning behind everything in this world.

Everything in the natural world is good, holy, and beautiful.

Misery and evil would soon vanish if only we had more faith in ourselves.

We close our eyes to
the world and then
cry out that it is dark.

**Do not let your epitaph read:
"It might have been…"**

Comfort is having something
to do, something to love,
someone to care for, and
something to hope for.

**There is opportunity to be
found in every difficulty if
you look hard enough.**

Character cannot be developed in ease and quiet. Only through experience of trial and suffering can the soul be strengthened, ambition inspired, and success achieved.

Helen Keller

We tend to choose to remain as we are, fearing that change is painful, when really it hurts far more going through life leaving things exactly as they are.

When we know what we're looking for, it is easier to see.

A person who is interested in other people is surrounded by friends, while the person who sits alone is waiting for others to become interested in him.

**The words we have spoken,
the past we have lived,
the opportunities that we neglected,
none of these can come back.**

When one door closes, another door opens.

Choose to live the life you deserve.

For the journey to begin, we must first take a step, and then a second.

Courage is not dangerous to us, but fear can be perilous.

When we fear someone or something, we give that person or thing power over us.

Many a dream has been murdered by security.

Never allow a day to pass
without practicing generosity.

**Never allow a day to pass
without enjoying life's
pleasures.**

The blacksmith's bellows breathe but they aren't alive.

We must learn to govern our sense, mind, and intellect.

We must choose to liberate ourselves from desire, fear, and anger.

Learn to accept yourself as you are; if you can't do that, then you can't expect anyone else to be able to.

Never negotiate out of fear.

We must accept that whatever we do at any time has the potential to anger somebody in some way.

I will not live in the continual fear that I might make a mistake.

Pride attaches undue importance to the superiority of one's status in the eyes of others.

I do not fear being wrong. That is what gives me my confidence.

None of us are inferior. We each have a part to play in life's infinite setup.

Act for yourself.

Face the truth.

A great many of us go to
our graves never knowing
what a great person we
might have been.

Our character is more important than our reputation.

Character is what we really are—our reputation is what others think we are.

Take charge of your life.
There is no need to ask
permission.

Never fear being inadequate.

Embrace the new,
respect the old.

When we choose to liberate ourselves from fear, we set a pattern for many others in our circle of friends and associates to follow.

Courage is the price that life exacts for granting peace. The soul that knows it not, knows no release from little things; knows not the livid loneliness of fear; nor mountain heights where bitter joy can hear the sound of wings.

Amelia Earhart

The light that frightens us most is the one that burns within us.

There is always something that is more important to us than fear.

Fear must not be left to rule us.

The moment we can do what we fear, our fear disappears.

Nobody is comfortable about doing something courageous. You have to be very frightened before you can show courage.

Accept who you are.

You, and only you,
are qualified to
judge yourself.

**Do not dwell upon what
you could become, unless
you are prepared to pay for
it with all that you are now.**

Shrug off the things that matter and you shrug off life.

Sound off about the things that matter and you embrace life.

In movement there is life.

We were born to celebrate the glorious gift of life that has been given to us.

There's no place like home.

Home is the place where
you feel accepted for
who you really are.

Where fear is, happiness is not.

The moment we begin to fear the opinions of others and hesitate to tell the truth that is in us, and from motives of policy are silent when we should speak, the divine floods of light and life no longer flow into our souls.

Elizabeth Cady Stanton

Are we comfortable enough with ourselves to reveal our insecurities to others?

Are we comfortable enough with other people to be content relating to them or do we feel compelled to dominate them?

Where thou art,
that is home.
Emily Dickinson

**There is no sanctuary of
virtue like home.**

Edward Everett

Happy is he who finds peace at home.

Home is the place where, when you have to go there, they have to take you in.

Robert Frost

A dearer, sweeter
spot than all the rest.
Robert Montgomery

**If a home is not a sanctuary
then it is not a home.**

Home is where
the heart is.
Pliny the Elder

**One may make the
house a palace of
sham, or he can
make it a home, a
refuge.**

Mark Twain

My home…It is my retreat and resting place from wars, I try to keep this corner as a haven against the tempest outside, as I do another corner in my soul.

Michel de Montaigne

Home, the spot of earth supremely blest.

All the good maxims
have been written.
It only remains to put
them into practice.

Blaise Pascal

Published by MQ Publications Limited
12 The Ivories, 6–8 Northampton Street
London N1 2HY
Tel: 020 7359 2244   Fax: 020 7359 1616
email: mail@mqpublications.com

Text © David Baird 2002
Design concept: Broadbase
Design: Philippa Jarvis

ISBN: 1-84072-409-9

1 3 5 7 9 10 8 6 4 2

Printed and bound in China